Farm Fields

Rocky Ravine

Sunny Clearing

Stream

Forest Places

To my parents and Elsbeth from Dorothy

The Wild Wonders Series is supported in part by Valerie Gates.

The animals and plants illustrated in this book are typical of eastern deciduous forests and have been reviewed and approved by scientists at the Denver Museum of Natural History.

We would like to thank Dr. Charles Preston, Curator of Ornithology at the Denver Museum of Natural History, for reviewing this book. His help and input at all stages of this project were invaluable.

Book design by Jill Soukup

International Standard Book Number 0-916278-71-9
Library of Congress Catalog Card Number 95-72984

Published by the Denver Museum of Natural History Press
2001 Colorado Boulevard, Denver, Colorado 80205
in cooperation with Roberts Rinehart Publishers
6309 Monarch Park Place, Niwot, Colorado 80503
(303) 652-2685

Distributed in the UK and Ireland by
Roberts Rinehart Publishers
Trinity House, Charleston Road
Dublin 6, Ireland

Distributed in the U.S. and Canada by Publishers Group West

Printed in Hong Kong

in the Forest

Ann Cooper

Illustrated by
Dorothy Emerling

Denver Museum of Natural History Press
Denver, Colorado

Wild
wonders
series

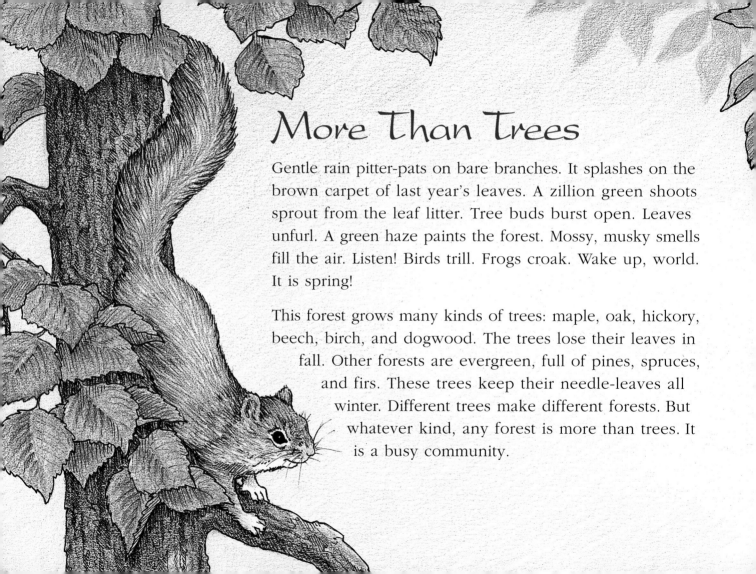

More Than Trees

Gentle rain pitter-pats on bare branches. It splashes on the brown carpet of last year's leaves. A zillion green shoots sprout from the leaf litter. Tree buds burst open. Leaves unfurl. A green haze paints the forest. Mossy, musky smells fill the air. Listen! Birds trill. Frogs croak. Wake up, world. It is spring!

This forest grows many kinds of trees: maple, oak, hickory, beech, birch, and dogwood. The trees lose their leaves in fall. Other forests are evergreen, full of pines, spruces, and firs. These trees keep their needle-leaves all winter. Different trees make different forests. But whatever kind, any forest is more than trees. It is a busy community.

Like sandwiches, forests have layers. Soil forms the bottom layer. Above the soil, dead leaves and fallen trees litter the forest floor. The next layer is called the understory. It has low shrubs and small trees. Tall trees form the top layer, called the canopy. By late spring, canopy leaves are so thick they shade the forest floor like an umbrella. The forest "sandwich" is home to all kinds of animals, from bugs to bears. Bats and skunks find food there. Snakes and salamanders seek shelter. Robins and squirrels build nests. Somebody uses every inch of forest, top to bottom. Look closely if you wish to peek into their secret lives!

Mouse's Tale

All winter, Mouse ate when she could. She found seeds and fallen grains of wheat at the farm field's edge. Mouse slept through storms. She shared her hollow-tree nest with other mice. Many bodies curled together are warmer than one body alone.

Once spring came, Mouse needed her own place to raise a family. Under cover of darkness, she went house hunting. She searched along tiny trails

and ran nimbly up and down in trees and bushes. Her tiny feet made no sound on damp leaves. Always, she listened mightily, ears twitching. What if Owl of the Silent Wings flew overhead?

Perfect! Mouse found an old bird's nest in a dogwood tree. She gathered twigs and grass to build a roof for the nest. She left a round front door and added a grass-and-feather lining for coziness.

A few mornings later her five pink babies were born. They were helpless, but they knew how to eat! Mouse Mother nursed them on her warm milk. When Mouse thought her babies had eaten enough, she moved away. The babies clung to her nipples. They would not let go! What appetites!

More About Mice

Homes

Woodland mice make nests in hollow trees, under logs or tree roots, or in abandoned birds' or squirrels' nests.

Beautiful Baby?

Newborn mice are wrinkly, squirmy, pink, and naked. Their eyes are closed and their ears are folded tight.

Mouse Math

A mother mouse has one to twelve babies in each litter (family). She may have four or more litters a year. Wow! That's a heap of babies.

Food

Mice eat beetles, slugs, snails, caterpillars, nuts, seeds, grain, fruit, and fruit pits. They nibble pits to get at the good food inside, leaving a neat, tooth-marked hole.

Housekeeping

Mice groom themselves to stay clean and neat, but they are very untidy housekeepers! Their old nests get so messy they have to keep moving to a new house!

Neighbors

Mice do not make trails. They use runways made by voles and shrews.

Growing Up

Mice are full grown at six weeks old. At eight weeks, they can have their own babies. Mice do not live long in the wild. Two years is old age for a mouse.

High Water

Woodland mice can swim well or climb into trees to escape floods!

Enemies

Owls, hawks, opossums, snakes, shrews, coyotes, foxes, weasels, skunks, bobcats, and domestic cats eat mice. Mice feed at night and prefer dark— not moonlit—nights, so their enemies can't see them.

Fawns in the Forest

Crrrr-ack! Mother Deer jerked up her head,
not finishing her mouthful of sweet elderberry
leaves. Her ears twitched this way and that to
hear danger. She sniffed the air. Her forest
clearing seemed safe. Perhaps a clumsy squirrel
had snapped a twig! But with two fawns just
one week old, hidden in the undergrowth, a
mother had to be extra careful!

Deer did not park her twins together. She told one fawn to hide in tall grass and ferns near a tree stump. The other fawn slept under a tangle of blackberry bushes. That way, a coyote would have less chance to harm both her babies. Mother stayed close by. She knew that if she huffed a warning, her fawns would freeze. They had no strong scent to give away their hideouts.

As light began to fade, robins and thrushes sang their evening songs. Deer stepped to a forest pool to drink. Her hooves left hollow prints like split hearts in the muddy bank. She wandered back to the clearing. She nibbled a leaf here, a tender shoot there. She sensed it was milk time for her fawns. One after the other, she fed them. They were still wobbly but grew stronger each day. Soon they would travel with her through the forest.

All About Deer

Antlers

Male deer (bucks) grow new antlers each year. During the fall mating season, bucks fight to win females. They use antlers as weapons to push and shove but rarely hurt each other.

They shed their antlers in winter.

Food

Deer eat green plants, even pond plants, in spring and summer. In the fall, they feast on acorns, beechnuts, and corn. Twigs of trees and shrubs are winter food.

Warning!

Deer raise their tails like white flags to confuse their enemies or warn other deer of danger.

Smelly Feet?

Deer prints smell musky from a body oil made between the deer's toes. The scent helps a deer sniff her way back to her fawns.

Neighbors

Rabbits, squirrels, and mice nibble shed deer antlers to get minerals.

Journeys

Deer follow well-worn trails through the forest as they feed each night. They stay active all year.

Fawns

Newborn fawns weigh about the same as most newborn humans. The fawns' speckled coats blend with dappled sun-and-shade patterns in the woods.

Family Life

Deer make no homes. Males and females stay apart except at mating. Males do not help raise the fawns. Fawns stay with their mother until she has her next family.

Enemies

Coyotes, bobcats, and humans hunt deer.

Bat's Night Out

The day had been hot. Even at dusk, the moist, mossy air hung like a heavy cloak. Bat woke slowly from her day's sleep. She stretched one wing, then the other. She took care not to dislodge the two babies clinging to her fur. She licked them and then groomed herself. Bat was hungry for juicy moths. But her babies were heavy. She could carry them and fly to a new roost if she had to. She preferred to hang them up at home and take a night out alone.

Dark came and along with it the first stars. Bat let go of her roost branch and as she dropped, she opened her long, pointed wings. *Swoosh!* No time to waste! She circled her clearing, sending high, clicking sounds into the night air. Her ears twitched and turned to pick up any sound-echoes bouncing off her prey.

Click. Echo. *Click, Click.* Echo, echo. Faster and faster the sounds bounced as Bat closed in on her prey. She swooped to catch a moth in her tail skin. Zap! With a flick, Bat tossed the moth into her mouth, neatly clipping off the scaly wings. Yum! Bat hunted long and hard through the buggy night. Her body needed to make milk for her babies, so she was always hungry!

More About Bats

Heads Down!

Bats hang upside down to roost (rest) by day. They cling tightly to a high branch by their hind feet. They look like bundles of leaves when they wrap their wings around their bodies.

Food

Bats hunt at night. They eat moths, mosquitoes, wasps, dragonflies, and beetles, which they catch as they fly. Bats bite off and drop insect legs and wings, which are heavy to carry and no good as food.

Grooming

Bats are clean animals. They comb their fur with their toenails and teeth and lick themselves clean like cats!

Drink
Bats fly low over ponds and streams, swooping down to sip a little water.

Winter
Some kinds of bats fly south in winter. Others hibernate (go into a deep sleep). When it is cold, few insects are left for them to eat.

Hunting Skills
Bats see well but hunt mostly by sound, not sight. They chirp. The high-pitched sounds bounce off insects as echoes. Bats figure out where prey is by how quickly the echoes return.

Voice
Some bats change their calls when they hunt near other kinds of bats so that their hunting echoes don't get muddled up. It is like tuning a radio to a new station!

Enemies
Bats' nighttime enemies are owls. By day, bats roost in trees, caves, or buildings where few predators can find them.

Dawn Chorus

Cheerily, cheer up, cheerily. Rosy half-light scarcely lit the forest, as Robin sang his morning song. Soon the woods filled to the brim with birdsong. Thrush whistled its clear, flutelike notes. Vireo sang nonstop, as if its breath would never end. Warbler sang a soft *weetsie weetsie.* Ovenbird called *teacher-teacher-teacher*, louder and louder. Even frogs joined the chorus, croaking ratchety love songs from the pond.

Robin and his mate were so-o busy that they took little notice of other forest birds—except other robins! Other robins wanted the same kind of nest places. They wanted the same kind of food. Other robin families were not good neighbors.

Robin sang loudly from his special tree when other robins came near. "This is my place. Keep out!" he tweeted in bird talk. Mother Robin collected mud from the stream bank to line her nest. She shaped the nest by sitting and scooting around. Then she laid her sky blue eggs.

Soon, five chicks hatched. Naked and squawking, they were all mouth! Robin brought them worms and insects, but the chicks were never full! As soon as they gobbled one treat, they opened wide mouths to chirp for more food!

Birds Galore!

Home Space

Birds divvy up the forest. Each species (kind) of bird uses a special kind of nest place—in the canopy or understory or on the ground. That way, they share an area of forest without fuss.

Wood Thrush

A female thrush makes a neat cup nest, lined with rootlets, in a tree. She builds for about five days. Then she lays her pale blue eggs and sits on them patiently, waiting for chick time.

Vireo

A vireo weaves a nest of grasses, vine tendrils, and strips of bark. The nest hangs between a Y-shaped twig. Vireos fasten the nest in place with spiders' silk!

Ovenbird

An ovenbird's ground nest has a round roof. The nest is the shape of an old-fashioned oven!

Warbler

Some warblers nest high in trees. The black-and-white warblers that sing *weetsie weetsie* make ground nests. The nests may be hidden under a log or in fallen leaves.

Enemies

Lots! Bobcats, foxes, raccoons, skunks, mice, chipmunks, squirrels, snakes, jays, magpies, and owls prey on eggs, nestlings, or adult birds. Hawks swoop to catch small birds as they fly.

Insect Eaters

Many woodland birds eat moths, butterflies, caterpillars, beetles, bugs, mosquitoes, and any small crawlies they find in the leaf litter or on leaves and bark.

Warning

Many birds have special calls, like the robin's rapid *tut tut tut* call, that warn of danger.

Opossum's Pocket

Mother Opossum had a pocket full of trouble!
Eight week ago, her bee-sized babies were born.
The babies climbed the wet trail she licked up
her belly to find a safe place in her fur-lined
pouch. They grabbed her nipples and began
to nurse . . . and grow . . . and nurse. Now the
nine babies were wriggly and restless. They no
longer nursed quietly as she went hunting each
night. They wanted out!

As dusk fell, Mother Opossum scrambled out of her grassy day bed. Three of her babies clambered out of her pouch to ride on her back. Opossum, her pink nose down, scratched along a leafy trail, snuffling. Black beetles—yum! Worms—delicious! Crickets, snails, a tasty stinkbug—Opossum gobbled up them all. Then she had a lucky find on a stream bank. It was a leftover dead rabbit. Opossum did not mind grabbing Fox's kill if Fox forgot it. Her babies sniffed the rabbit curiously. They had not learned about meat yet!

Suddenly, Fox returned. Opossum's babies tumbled into her pouch. Opossum showed her fifty teeth in a fierce grin. She hissed and drooled. Fox came closer. Opossum gave up the rabbit and scurried into a tangle of brambles. What a lucky escape with her pouch full of babies!

Opossum Facts

Food

Opossums eat almost anything, including dead animals, insects, fruit, veggies, worms, snails, crayfish, salamanders, frogs, eggs, mice, dog food, and even garbage!

Homes

Opossums use dens in hollow trees, under logs, or in brush piles. They have several dens and use the one nearest to where they happen to be at daybreak. They line the dens with grass and leaves, which they carry with their tails.

Enemies

Foxes, coyotes, bobcats, dogs, and great horned owls prey on opossums.

Stinkers?

Do you know that skunks spray their enemies? Opossums don't make spray, but their bodies smell like dead fish. Phew! That puts off their enemies!

Tails

Grown opossums curl their ratlike, hairless tails around branches as safety belts when they walk or sit in trees. Only young opossums are light enough to hang by their tails.

Babies

Opossums can have five to thirteen babies. The young leave the pouch when they are chipmunk-sized. At four months, the young are on their own!

Toe-thumbs

Opossums have thumb-like toes on their hind feet. They use their "toe-thumbs" to pick up and grip things.

Playing Dead

An opossum plays dead when it can't escape. It flops on one side, eyes and mouth half open, still as death. It poops smelly droppings.

Predators think they have found a rotting body, and move on. The opossum does not decide to play dead. Its body does these things from fright.

Salamander's Story

All day, warm summer rain misted through the woods. Drops formed and plopped from every fern and leaf tip. Water trickled in the once-dry streambed. By nightfall, skies cleared and fireflies flickered in the clearing. Salamander slithered from under her rock. She ambled down to a low, muddy place to find a male. They circled one another, nudging and bobbing, deciding to mate.

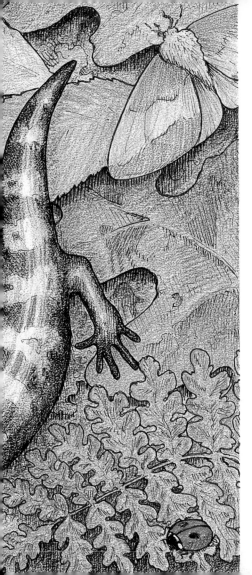

Later, Salamander found a small hollow in the mud. It was sheltered by a fallen log. She laid more than a hundred eggs and curled her body over them to protect them. She did not want her eggs to dry out. She did not want shrews or beetles to eat them.

In the next week more rain fell. Salamander's muddy place became a small pond. She left her nest and slithered back to the woods. Her mothering task was over. The eggs washed into the water. Salamander was far away, hidden under a rock, when her babies (larvae) hatched. She never saw her family. The larvae, little wigglers with feathery gills, stayed in the pond all winter. They grew fat on water insects and worms.

Salamander Facts

Amphibian

Salamanders change as they grow up. Eggs hatch into water-living larvae. Larvae grow, leave the pond in early summer, and live on land as adults. Because of their water-land habits, salamanders are called amphibians.

They may live in dry, shady areas part of the time but must return to wet places to lay eggs.

Families

Marbled salamanders are unlike many other kinds of salamander, because they lay eggs in late summer. In dry years, the eggs may not hatch until spring.

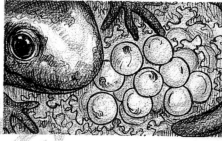

Slime

Slimy skin helps the salamander breathe and keeps the animal from drying out and dying.

Food

Adult salamanders eat worms, insects, slugs, and small frogs. Young salamander larvae eat pond insects.

Neighbors

Salamanders lead secret lives. Their insect and small mammal neighbors may never know they are there!

Enemies

Raccoons, snakes, opossums, and other streamside hunters— even bears—may catch salamanders. Turtles, newts, and dragonfly larvae may eat some salamander larvae.

Winter

Adult salamanders spend the wintertime hidden beneath leaf litter, in rock crevices, or underground in vole or gopher burrows. As the weather cools, their bodies cool. They don't move or eat until spring.

Night Is for Hunters

Screech Owl blinked his eyes sleepily. Time to get up. It was nearly night. He stretched one feathery leg, then the other, opening and closing his talons (claws). He opened and closed his wings, shaking the feathers into place. *Thump.* What was that? Owl turned his head almost all round to see behind him. It was only a squirrel—nothing to worry about.

Owl pecked and poked his breast feathers, working them smooth with his beak. Burp! Owl spat up a pellet of fur and bones—the remains of last night's meal. He felt lighter, ready for the hunt. On silent wings, he swooped through the clearing, listening for mouse sounds. He liked dry nights, when mouse steps crackled in fallen leaves.

Who-huh-who-who-who, called a great horned owl. Screech Owl flew to a perch in a leafy oak and kept silent. He waited until the big owl glided away across the distant farm fields—waited for safe hunting again.

A white-lined, shadowy shape wandered along the stream bank, scratching and digging. Screech Owl wanted nothing to do with a skunk! But as the skunk shuffled along, it stirred up moths and crickets chilled by the cool air. Owl swooped down and ate.

More About Owls

Family Life

Screech owl parents raise four or five young in a tree-hole nest (first made and used by woodpeckers). The mother warms and hatches the eggs. Babies are white and fluffy. Both parents bring food to the chicks. Chicks fly about a month after they hatch.

What Big Eyes...

Owls have huge eyes to see moving prey even in dim light. Both eyes face front, like our eyes, so the owl can judge distances when hunting.

What Big Ears...

Those tufts may look like ears, but they are feathery decorations that help owls recognize each other. Hearing ears lie under feathers at each side of an owl's head.

Feet and Feathers

Talons—sharp tools for catching prey—are curved and strong. Wing feathers have soft, fringed edges. They make almost no sound as the owl flies and hunts.

Voice

A screech owl's voice can send shivers up your spine. It is a warbling, wailing noise like the whinny of a ghost horse.

Food

Screech owls eat shrews, mice, and insects. Less often they eat frogs, toads, small bats, and salamanders.

Enemies

Large owls and hawks hunt small owls. Snakes may eat owl eggs or young. An owl freezes if startled during the day. Its shape and color make it look like a dead branch.

Little birds often "mob" perched owls when they find them in daylight. What a fuss! The little birds look as if they are saying, "Get out of here!"

Neighbors

Flying squirrels do not really fly. They glide with skin-flap parachutes.

The Waiting Game

The first snow of winter had fallen, wet and mushy. Bobcat lay in a favorite outcrop of rocks. Tonight, her kittens would learn for the first time about cold and white. Her kittens were five months old—quite grown up! She had taught them well. She no longer brought them live mice to let them practice hunting. They caught food for themselves—well, most of the time! But in the snow? That might be harder.

Bobcat stretched, flexed her claws, and licked her fur with her rough tongue. At dusk, she set out. Her three kittens followed. They kept the white spots on the back of Mother's ears in sight, so they would not get lost. They walked stealthily, just like their mother.

Cottontails were easy to see against the snow. But Mother Bobcat knew they stayed near their escape holes. She must stalk them silently and pounce. Could her fidgety kittens do that, not yet knowing snow? Snow muffled sound. But a spotted coat showed more in snow than in the dappled summer forest. What should they do? Would it be better to climb into a tree above the rabbit trail and play the waiting game?

Bobcat Facts

Families

Bobcats can have one to six babies. They usually have two or three.

Male bobcats do not help raise the kittens. The kittens stay with their mother until they are about nine months old, sometimes longer. Bobcats can live to be ten to twelve years old.

Night Vision

In bright light, the centers (pupils) of a bobcat's eyes are slit-like. After dark, the pupils open wide to gather the dim light. Bobcats can see well enough to hunt by night.

Tracks

Bobcats walk on their toes. Their tracks show no claw marks because the claws retract (pull in) like a cat's claws.

Enemies

Bobcats have few enemies except dogs and people, but kittens are hunted by foxes, coyotes, eagles, and large owls.

Names

Bobcats are sometimes called wildcats.

Keep Out Signs

A bobcat marks its home space with piles of scat (droppings), scratched trees, and urine. The scent marks tell other bobcats to "keep out." It is the bobcats' way of sharing space without fighting.

Fine Fur Coat

In summer, a bobcat's coat is tawny brown. The bobcat molts (sheds) this coat and grows a thicker, grayer coat for winter.

Food

Bobcats hunt mice, rats, rabbits, shrews, squirrels, opossums, cats, deer and fawns, and ground birds—even turkeys!

Cottontail's Escape

One morning, Cottontail stayed out later than usual. He liked to tuck safely under the briars before the day got too bright. But the first hard frost had killed most of the tender woodland plants. Food was getting harder to find.

Cottontail hoppity-hopped over tree roots to a small sumac tree. He nibbled the bark. When he heard a rustling in the fallen

leaves, he sat up tall to look. It was a squirrel, burying nuts for winter. Nuts were no good to Cottontail. He hopped past the forest edge to the farm field, looking for wheat stalks or clover. Just as he started eating, his wary, side-facing eyes saw a shadowy shape. The shape was loping toward him. Fox!

Cottontail ran a zigzag path through the wheat stalks. He ran as fast as his hoppity legs could go. Fox followed. In his fright, Cottontail forgot which way led home. He ran for his life. He changed his path this way and that, trying to outrun Fox. Cottontail's ears lay flat with fear. Suddenly, he stumbled into a small hole. It led to a narrow, cobwebby tunnel, with no smells of an owner. He scurried deep inside—away from Fox—before he stopped to catch his breath. His heart pounded, his whiskers quivered. But this time he was safe.

More About Rabbits

Home for Babies

A mother rabbit digs a shallow nest in the ground to get ready for her babies. She lines the nest with grass and bits of fur that she plucks from her belly.

Babies

Newborn rabbits are naked or have soft fur. Their eyes are closed. Their mother nurses them at dawn and dusk. When she leaves, she covers them with grass and fur to hide them. A female rabbit may raise four families in a year.

Bunny Hop

When rabbits run, the small front feet make two round prints, then the two large back feet overtake them and make two large prints in front. Can you figure out which way this rabbit was hopping?

Food

Rabbits eat many kinds of green plants, but they especially like clover, dandelions, and wheat. In winter they eat tree bark, buds, and twigs.

Poop-eater!

Rabbits have two kinds of scat (droppings)—soft and dry. Rabbits eat their soft droppings. It's a second chance to get nourishment from food.

How Old?

A rabbit's life is full of dangers. Rabbits *can* live a few years, but most of them live only a few months.

Enemies

Lots! Hawks, owls, crows, weasels, dogs, cats, snakes, bobcats, foxes, and coyotes all prey on rabbits.

Winter

Rabbits do not hibernate. During winter storms, they may shelter underground in an old woodchuck burrow and skip a night's meal. They must feed when the snow stops because they have no food stored away.

Animals All Around

Animals like to live their lives privately. Every wild place you go, there are many more animals than you see. Perhaps the animals are watching you! Here are some more forest animals. Did you find them as you read this book?

Black Bears

Bears eat grass, berries and fruits, seeds, nuts, tree roots, and bark. They hunt for small prey—insects, mice, fish, frogs, birds' eggs, and dead animals. Bears love honey and raid wild bees' nests to get it. They usually stay away from people.

This print is from a bear cub's front foot.

Squirrels

Squirrels bury stores of nuts and acorns for the winter and find some of them by smell. The rest sprout the next spring—new trees for the forest.

Raccoons

These animals hunt for small fish and crayfish in ponds and streams. They feel their prey with their sensitive fingers.

Flying Squirrels
At night, flying squirrels glide from tree to tree using skin-flap parachutes.

Foxes
Red foxes and gray foxes live in the forest. Both hunt small animals and insects. Gray foxes climb trees.

Frogs
Frogs find mates by croaking. Each species (kind) of frog sings its own song.

Skunks
Skunks squirt their smelly spray to keep away enemies.

Did You Find?
Chipmunk
Vole
Woodchuck
Blue jay
Great horned owl
Turkey
Chickadee
Garter snake
Painted turtle
Wood frog
Swallowtail butterfly
Luna moth
Rosy maple moth
Dragonfly
Beetles, bugs, and bees

Forest Sandwich?

Many animals share the layers of the forest. The animals use each leaf, rock, bush, hole, and fallen tree. Animals may stay in one layer. They may move between layers to find homes or food.

▲ Some animals prefer the sunny canopy.

▲ Some animals prefer the damp, shady understory.

▲ Many small creatures live on the leafy forest floor or down in the soil.

It takes all of the animals in all of the layers to complete the links of life in the forest.

Canopy

Bat

Owl

Bird

Understory

Bobcat

Deer

Opossum

Mouse

Forest Floor

Cottontail

Salamander

Soil Layer

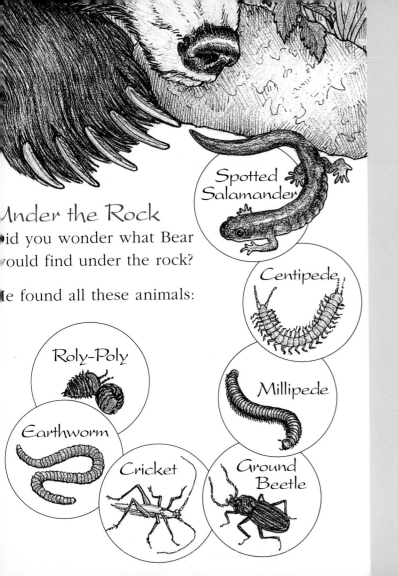

Under the Rock

Did you wonder what Bear would find under the rock?

He found all these animals:

Spotted Salamander

Centipede

Roly-Poly

Millipede

Earthworm

Cricket

Ground Beetle

Tracks

Did you notice tracks on some pages? They are life-size. Measure them with your hand to test the size of the animals' feet.

Treasure Maps

Front map: Find the stream where Opossum found Fox's leftover rabbit. Find the rocky ravine where Bobcat and her kittens rested.

Back map: Which animal finds food in the farm fields? Which animal uses the smallest space? Who comes to the pond to lay eggs?

Babies

Animals have babies in many ways. Do you remember which parents had which babies?
- A jelly-egg that hatched into a larva?
- A tiny baby that crawled into a pouch?
- A pale blue egg that hatched into a chick?
- A spotted baby that hid in the woods?

Links of Life

The forest is a like a city for creatures. It has homes for all kinds of animals. Some live in the "high-rise" canopy; some choose the damp, musky "ground floor." Others live in the forest "basement"—the soil. The forest has places for them to eat, drink, and hide.

Just as a city changes with homes being built and torn down, a forest keeps changing, too. Trees die. Woodpeckers chisel out nests in the dead wood. Sometimes owls or squirrels take over the holes. In time, the trees fall, leaving sunny clearings that suit deer and cottontails. Fallen logs become

hiding places for salamanders and chipmunks. New trees, bushes, and vines sprout and grow. Soon, the tangled layer is full of birds' nests.

Year after year, a whole network of animals lives in the forest. They are hunters and hunted. They are parents and young. They are furry, or feathery, or scaly, or slimy. They are small and large. They need each other and the forest. And each one is an important link in the whole pattern of nature.

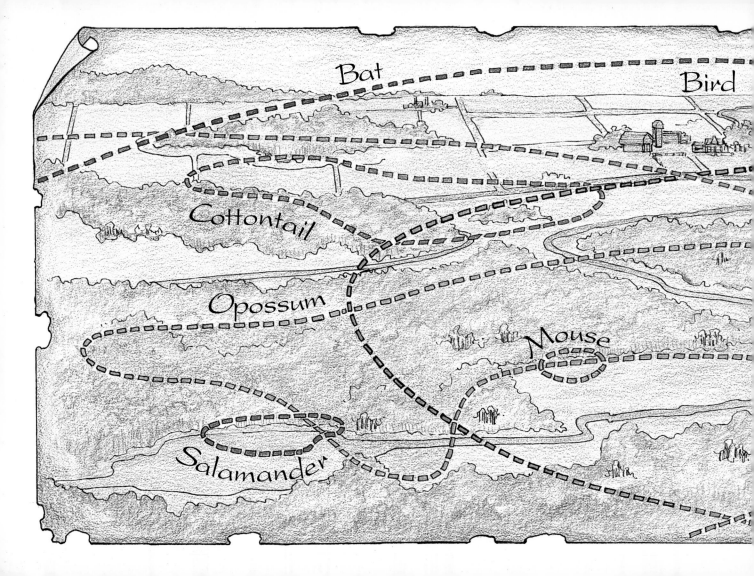